Death Match

Andy Croft

For Sveta, Oleg and Elena

First published 2011 by A & C Black,
an imprint of Bloomsbury Publishing Plc
50 Bedford Square, London WC1B 3DP

www.acblack.com

ISBN 978-1-4081-4263-9

A CIP catalogue for this book is available from the British Library.

This book is produced using paper that is made from wood
grown in managed, sustainable forests. It is natural, renewable
and recyclable. The logging and manufacturing processes conform
to the environmental regulations of the country of origin.

Printed and bound in Great Britain
by CPI Cox and Wyman, Reading, RG1 8EX

recommended by

www.catchup.org

Catch Up is a not-for-profit charity which
aims to address the problem of
underachievement that has its roots in
literacy and numeracy difficulties.

DEATH MATCH

Contents

Chapter 1

Losing

June 1942

"I'm starving," Misha groaned.

"Me too," I said.

Me and Misha were very hungry.

Of course, boys are always hungry. But this was different. Everyone in the city was hungry. There was no food in the shops. Most of the shops were shut.

"We had potato soup yesterday," Misha went on.

"So did we," I said.

"I'm sick of potatoes."

"Me too," I grumbled.

But what would we do when the potatoes ran out? All the cats and dogs had been eaten a long time ago. People were cooking mice and rats now. Some people were eating soup made from grass.

Misha's family lived in the same block as ours. We were in the same class at school. (Only, we hadn't been to school for over six months. All the schools were closed or burned down.)

We were both football mad. Misha was a really good goalie. I played left-back.

When we grew up, we wanted to play for our local club, Dynamo Kiev. It was the best team in Ukraine. It was one of the best teams in the whole Soviet Union. But that was before the War.

Don't ever let anyone tell you that war is a game. It isn't. Football is a game.

But even football can be more than just a game.

Chapter 2

Shooting

Last year, in June 1941, Nazi Germany invaded the Soviet Union. In just a few weeks the German armies reached our city, Kiev.

We fought back, of course. There was shooting in the streets. Bodies everywhere. Kiev was in flames. But we lost. By the end of the battle, half a million of our soldiers were missing – dead or taken prisoner.

Both our dads were missing. We didn't know if they were still alive.

Misha's brother was with our soldiers who hid in the woods and fought the Nazis. We wanted to join them when we were older.

The Nazis turned Kiev into a prison. No-one was allowed to leave the city. We had to stay indoors between six o'clock at night and five o'clock in the morning. Everyone was hungry. Even the hospitals were closed.

Every day the Nazis took people to the train station and sent them to work as slaves in Germany.

Then there were the shootings. The Nazis dragged men out of their homes and shot them in the street. They took thousands of people to a wood called Babin Yar. None of them ever came back.

Misha's mum had heard that the Nazis were going to shoot all the men over 15. Me and Misha were 14. We would soon be 15.

* * *

"Let's look for something to eat," Misha said.

"Like what?" I said.

"Let's try the bread shop. Maybe we can find some old bread in the bins."

The shop made bread for the Nazis. It wasn't very far away, so we could get there and back before six o'clock. We kept to the back streets. We didn't want to meet a German patrol.

Half of the houses in Kiev were in ruins. The walls were black with smoke. The windows were broken. The roads were full of rubble.

We both stopped when we were near the bread shop. We could hear shouting in the yard behind the shop.

There were people playing football.

Chapter 3

Training

We peered through the gates. Some men were kicking a football in the yard. They were wearing work clothes. But this wasn't just a kick-around. These players were good.

One of the players trapped the ball under his foot, flicked it up and belted it towards the goal. The goalie threw himself across the goal and tipped it over the wall.

"Great save!" yelled Misha. I ran after the ball and kicked it back over the gate. The goalie caught it.

"Thanks!" he said.

Then we saw who he was – Kolya, the Dynamo Kiev goalie!

We looked round at the other players. Half the Dynamo team were in the yard.

The game was over. The players were going inside.

Kolya turned to us.

"You had better go home, lads," he said. "The Nazis are on the look-out for kids stealing bread."

"But Kolya – what are you doing here?"
I asked.

"I work here. The boss found me on the street. I had just been let out of the prison camp. He gave me a job here, sweeping the yard. He lets me sleep here as well. It's better than starving, or going to Babin Yar to be shot."

He went on, "When the Nazis let the others out of the prison camp, I found jobs for them here too. You see," he grinned, "we're starting a football team. We call ourselves Start FC. We have been training after work."

"But who will you play against?" asked Misha.

"The Nazis," said Kolya.

"The Nazis? But – "

"They're starting a league," said Kolya.

"But they are the enemy!" said Misha. "You can't play football with the Nazis. They are killing people all over the city, every day!"

Kolya nodded. "Of course they are the enemy," he said. "One day we'll drive them out of Kiev. We're going to start by beating them at football. It will give the people something to cheer about.

"We've even found some shirts," he told us. "Red, like our country's flag. We don't have guns, but we can still fight the Nazis on the football field! The first game is next Sunday, at the Dynamo Stadium. Tell everyone about it. We want a big crowd. I hope you'll be there."

Misha and I looked at each other. Nothing would stop us!

"Catch!" said Kolya, as he threw something over the wall. Misha jumped up and caught it. It was a loaf of bread.

"Good save!" shouted Kolya.

Chapter 4

Flying Start

On Sunday, there was a big crowd. It was really hot, and the game was free. It felt like a holiday. Except that there were Nazi soldiers all over the city.

The other teams in the league were made up of soldiers from Germany, Romania and Hungary. But in the first game, Start was playing another Kiev team.

The German soldiers took all the seats. Everyone else had to stand. Me and Misha sat on the grass by the touch-line with the other kids.

When the teams ran out, we looked at each other. We were worried. The other team all had boots but some of the Start players were only wearing shoes. The other team looked younger and fitter.

"Come on, Start!" we shouted.

There was no need to worry. Our players were much better. The other team couldn't get the ball. The Start players ran rings round them. The crowd cheered every time a Start player got the ball.

Then the goals started coming. 1–0. 2–0. 3–0. 4–0. 5–0. Easy!

Every time the ball went out of the ground, all the kids raced to bring it back. Once I got it and threw it to Kolya for a goal-kick.

"Thanks," he said, with a big smile.

In the end we won 7–2. The crowd went wild. But the Nazis did not look happy.

Chapter 5

Foul

A few days later, we were playing football with some of the other kids. Misha was in goal. He kicked the ball out. It sailed down the street and hit a bald man on the head.

He glared at us, then he picked up the ball.

It was old Rat-face, who lived on the top floor of our block. He used to teach at our school. Everyone called him Rat-face because of his sticky-out teeth.

We were scared of him. You see, there were some people in Kiev who liked the Nazis. Not many, but enough to make trouble.

Maybe they wanted to be Nazis. Maybe they hoped that the Nazis would give them jobs. But people like Rat-face made friends with the Nazis by helping them.

"Sorry, sir," I said. "It won't happen again."

He glared at me. "I might have known *you* would be involved," he said. "You're as bad as your father."

"My father is a hero," I said. "He's fighting with our army."

"Your father is probably dead," he said.

He bent his ugly face close to mine and went on:

"Keep out of my way. I can make big trouble for you. Know what I mean?"

I nodded.

Then he marched off, still holding our ball.

"He's evil," said Misha. "My mum said that he told the Nazis where some Jews were hiding. The Nazis rounded up the Jews and they were all shot."

"Let's keep out of his way," I said.

Chapter 6

Winning

Two weeks later FC Start played their next game. It was another easy win. The other team scored twice. Both their goals were miles offside, but the ref gave them.

We still won. 6–2.

Two weeks later we played again. 11–0. Magic.

Then we played a German team. 9–1! The Start players were scoring for the fun of it.

The next game was against a German army side and we won – 6–0!

Two days later Start had to play again. The players looked tired. They were playing another army team. The soldiers were fitter and faster.

But we still won, 5–1.

The army team wanted a re-match the next Sunday.

The Nazis wanted to stop Start supporters from getting in to the game, so they started charging people to come in. But the crowd was the biggest yet.

Misha and I climbed over the fence.

It was the hardest game so far, but we still won. 3–2.

At last we had something to cheer about. So did the city. Everyone was talking about FC Start. Seven wins out of seven!

During the games we tried to forget about the War. But of course we couldn't. Our soldiers were still fighting the enemy. And our footballers were fighting them on the pitch.

The Nazis weren't cheering.

The next game was against the German air-force team. Everyone said they were very good. But the Nazis knew they could only win by cheating.

They kicked our players, tackled late and pulled our players' shirts. The Nazis were going for the man, not the ball.

But we stuffed them. 5–1!

Eight games played, eight games won. Come on, Start!

Chapter 7

Counter-attack

When we walked in to Misha's flat, a man was sitting at the kitchen table, smoking. There was a gun on the table in front of him. As we came in he jumped to his feet, the gun in his hand.

"It's OK, Max," said Misha. "It's only us." He turned to me. "You know my brother, don't you?"

Of course I knew Max. Everyone in our street knew Max. We knew that he was one of our soldiers in the woods.

"Max has brought us some food," said Misha. "More potatoes!"

"But how did you get here?" I asked Max. "If the Germans catch you – "

"We have ways of getting into the city," said Max. "It's getting out that's hard. The German patrols are everywhere."

"Max is here for the football," said Misha.

"Football?" I was confused. "Have you come to watch FC Start?"

"Start have a re-match with the air-force team tomorrow," said Max. "Lots of top Nazis are going to be in the city for the game. We are going to blow up the hotel where they are staying. We'll show the Nazis that they haven't beaten us yet. We can still fight!"

I was scared. Every time our soldiers killed a German soldier, the Nazis shot a hundred people. Not long ago, our soldiers cut some phone cables, and the Nazis shot four hundred men.

But what else could we do? The Nazis were going to kill us all anyway.

Chapter 8

Defending

It was the day of the re-match. Tonight Max and the other soldiers were going to blow up the hotel.

Max was in Misha's kitchen, with a large black bag over his shoulder.

"I'd like to come to the game with you," he said. "But I have work to do. Enjoy the game for me!"

We almost bumped into old Rat-face on the landing.

"Oi!" he shouted. "Watch where you're going!"

We ran down the stairs. We didn't want to be late for the game.

It looked as if there was going to be a big crowd. The Nazis had put up posters all over the city. "Revenge!" said the posters.

This time the Nazis meant to win. Even the ref was German.

There were Nazis everywhere. A lot of them had dogs. The dogs kept barking at the crowd.

What if the Nazis won? Or worse – what if Start won again? What would the Nazis do then?

We were just about to climb the fence into the ground when a German soldier came round the corner. We hid behind a pillar.

The soldier was talking to Rat-face. He was pointing back towards our street.

We heard, "Soldiers … hotel … blow up … arrest …"

He gave the soldier Misha's address.

We forgot all about the game. We ran
back to Misha's flat as fast as we could.

When we passed some German soldiers, we slowed down. We didn't want them to ask what we were doing. As soon as we reached the corner we started running again.

We just reached the flat in time to find Max.

"Max – you have got to hide the bombs. The Germans are coming! Old Rat-face has told them you are here," I panted.

Max picked up the black bag.

"Right," he said. "I know just the place to hide them."

He grinned. "You two had better get back. The Nazis will be here any minute."

We shook hands.

"Be quick," said Max, "or you will miss the game."

Chapter 9

Revenge

We raced back to the stadium and climbed over the fence. The game was about to start. We sat on the grass by the touch-line.

When the teams came out we knew there was going to be trouble. The Start players refused to give the Nazi salute before kick-off. The Nazis looked very cross.

As soon as the game started we knew the Nazi plan. They were going to play dirty again. Our players were chopped down all over the pitch.

Kolya made a save at the feet of a Nazi forward, and he kicked Kolya in the head. The ref waved 'play on'.

While Kolya was still on the floor, the Germans scored. 1–0 to the enemy.

The ref was ignoring all the fouls. But at last Start were given a free kick. Vanya stepped up to take it.

Bang! 1–1.

The soldiers with dogs moved into the crowd. Things were looking ugly.

By half-time we were winning 3–1.

Later Kolya told us that a Nazi officer went into the Start changing room at half-time. He told them to let the Germans win – or else. They knew what he meant.

Both sides scored twice in the second half. It was 5–3.

Then Sasha got the ball. He beat one man. Then another. Then another. He took it round the German keeper, but then he stopped the ball on the goal-line.

Sasha grinned, turned round, and kicked the ball back towards the centre circle.

The crowd cheered and started laughing at the Nazis.

There were still several minutes left, but the ref blew the whistle. 5–3 to us.

The Nazis had called it the Revenge Match. This was our revenge.

Chapter 10

Own Goal

After the game we ran back home. There was a German truck outside our block. Rat-face was outside, talking to a Nazi. He looked pleased with himself.

Some small kids were kicking a ball. We joined in, all the time watching the block. What if they found Max? What if they found the bombs?

After a few minutes more Nazis came out. They started shouting at Rat-face. He looked worried. Then they took him inside. We could see them at the window of Rat-face's flat. There was more shouting.

After a few minutes they came out again. One of the Nazis was carrying Max's large black bag.

Max must have put it in Rat-face's flat. He was in real trouble now!

The Nazis made Rat-face stand against a
wall. He was trying to say something. The
Nazis raised their guns. Rat-face went down
on his knees.

Just then one of the kids passed me the ball. I swung my leg and I shot it as hard as I could against the wall.

Bang!

Chapter 11

Victory

A few days later, the Nazis arrested our players.

They took the players to a prison camp outside the city, not far from Babin Yar.

Then they shot Kolya, Vanya and Sasha. Some people said they were still wearing their football shirts when they died.

The Nazis thought they had won. But early next year, our army smashed the German army. By the end of that year, we had kicked the Nazis out of Kiev.

By 1945 our army was in the German capital, and Hitler was dead.

We found out later that both our dads were killed back in 1941. Max died in the last months of the war.

* * *

Misha and I are old men now. Of course we still watch Dynamo. Before every home game we stop outside the stadium and look at the statue there. It's in memory of the heroes of FC Start. Our heroes.

Dynamo are now one of the best football clubs in the world. We have reached the semi-finals of the Champions League three times. One day we will win it.

Lots of famous clubs have come here to play Dynamo. We have had lots of great players over the years. But none as great as the heroes of FC Start.

In every game you have to know when to attack and when to defend. The Dynamo players could have let the Nazis win. Perhaps they should have done.

But which is worse – cheating to win, or cheating to lose?

Our team played for their city and their freedom. They lost their lives. But they won the game.

What would you have done?